POPE JOHN PAUL II

POPE JOHN PAUL II

REFLECTIONS ON THE MAN

Walter J. Ziemba

Paulist Press
New York/Mahwah, N.J.

English translation of Pope John Paul II's writings as well as public speeches, homilies, and addresses are taken from the official website of the Holy See, www.vatican.va.

Cover and book design by Lynn Else

Front cover photograph copyright © 2000 by Grzegorz Galazka. Used by permission of the photographer. All rights reserved.

Repeating photo of the statue of Pope John Paul II (commissioned by Holy Cross Church in Romania, 1997) by Silviu Bejan. Used by permission of the artist. Visit http://www.members.shaw.ca/sbejan0978/.

Back cover photograph copyright © 2004 by Servizio Fotographico de "L'O.R." 00120 Città del Vaticano. Used by permission of the author.

Library of Congress Cataloging-in-Publication Data

Ziemba, Walter.
    Pope John Paul II : reflections on the man / Walter J. Ziemba.
        p. cm.
    ISBN 0-8091-4364-X (alk. paper)
    1. John Paul II, Pope, 1920–2005. 2. Catholic Church—Church history—20th century. I. Title.
    BX1378.5.Z56 2005
    282'.092—dc22

                                                                                2005011939

Published by Paulist Press
997 Macarthur Boulevard
Mahwah, New Jersey 07430

www.paulistpress.com

Printed and bound in the
United States of America

DEDICATED

WITH

LOVE, GRATITUDE, AND ADMIRATION

TO

HIS HOLINESS

POPE JOHN PAUL II

Contents

The Holy Father

The Roman Pontiff, as the successor of Peter, is the perpetual and visible principle and foundation of unity of both the bishops and of the faithful.

—*Lumen gentium,* 23

Introduction

In 1969 Pope John Paul II, then Cardinal Karol Wojtyla, visited the United States and the American Polonia (Polish-Americans). How did this visit come about?

In December 1967 I was appointed the head of the Orchard Lake Schools in Michigan. One of the first things I did was to plan a trip to Poland for the summer of 1968 to invite Cardinal Stefan Wyszynski to visit the Polonia of the United States. Our visit with the cardinal was most pleasant and profitable, but when the invitation to come to the United States was extended to him, he declined, saying that he had to stay in Poland to "watch the store." He was afraid that if he left the country, the government might never allow him to return. But he did make a suggestion: there was a young cardinal in Krakow (in fact, at the time he was the youngest cardinal in the world), Karol Wojtyla. Invite him, and he might come.

The visit with Cardinal Karol Wojtyla was most memorable. In the course of the conversation during lunch, I extended the invitation and used the authority of Cardinal Wyszynski as the clincher. Cardinal Wojtyla listened with great interest; he understood the purpose of the visit as a contact between the Polish hierarchy and the American Polonia and said, "*Zobaczymy*—we shall see."

More or less at the same time, the cardinal received another invitation to the North American continent from the Polish Canadian Congress to help them celebrate their twenty-fifth anniversary. Soon after, he accepted both invitations, and both Polonias began to make plans for his visit.

Cardinal Wojtyla arrived in Montreal on August 28, 1969. From there he traveled to Quebec, back to Montreal, to Ottawa, Calgary, Edmonton, Winnipeg, Toronto, Hamilton, Burlington, London, Woodstock, back to Toronto, and then to Ottawa and Niagara Falls, Ontario.

On September 16 he crossed over to Buffalo, New York, and then visited Hartford, New Britain, Cleveland, Pittsburgh, Detroit, Hamtramck, Orchard Lake, Boston, Washington, D.C., Baltimore, St. Louis, Chicago, Philadelphia, Doylestown, Brooklyn, New York, Lodi, and back to New York, from where he departed for Rome on October 1. It was a whirlwind trip that covered seventeen cities in sixteen days. He never missed an event, a flight, or a trip. We took him to all the major centers of the American Polonia and were able to meet all of the American cardinals except Cardinal McIntyre in Los Angeles because of the additional distance.

The cardinal's second trip to the United States came in 1976, when he attended the International

Eucharistic Congress in Philadelphia. The Orchard Lake Schools had invited the cardinal and nineteen other bishops from Poland for a three-day conference on the subject of the American Polonia on the campus of the schools. The cardinal and the bishops learned a lot about the American Polonia from the papers that were presented on the subject chosen by the cardinal: "What can Poland do for the Polonia, and what can Polonia do for Poland?" The chairman of the conference was Cardinal Wojtyla, who led the discussions and drafted a long list of conclusions to be implemented in the future. The bond between the Church in Poland and the American Polonia was permanently established. On this trip the cardinal stayed forty-five days and visited fourteen cities.

Both of the cardinal's trips taught him much about the American Polonia and the United States. He was a keen observer, an accurate analyst, a sharp questioner, and an ultimate diplomat. The style of his visits was that of the pastoral visits of bishops in Poland. He wanted to meet everyone. He met thousands. All remembered his visits, and when he was elected pope, these same thousands were able to say, "I met him! I have a picture with him!" Providence had prepared the future pope for his papal pastoral visits to the United States and to the American Polonia.

A Man of Love,
Faith, and Hope

This is the "acceptable time"…so that the Lord will

hasten the arrival of the moment when we can live in

full communion together in the celebration of the Holy

Eucharist, and thus to contribute more effectively so

that the world believes that Jesus Christ is Lord.

—Letter of John Paul II to the ecumenical patriarch
of Constantinople, November 27, 2004

"*Niech bedzie pochwalony Jezus Chrystus!*" ("Praised be Jesus Christ!").

This is the traditional Polish religious greeting that Pope John Paul II used to greet groups and it captures the theme of his life and papacy. May Jesus Christ be praised—always, everywhere, in every prayer, in every thought and action, in every aspiration and decision. May God be glorified: Father, Son, and Holy Spirit. "Whatever you do in word or in work, may it give praise to the Lord."

How do you summarize, encapsulate, synthesize a modern papacy after nearly twenty-seven years, the second longest in history (after Blessed Pope Pius IX, and not including Saint Peter's reign of thirty-three years)? How do you capture the essence, the personality, the heart and soul of a teacher-mystic who is already being called "John Paul *the Great*"? How do you speak in one language about a man who spoke so many different languages, especially the language of love? How do you discern the many themes of his writings, his addresses, his allocutions, his apostolic letters, his encyclicals, and his inspiring Sunday Angelus messages? How do you portray his manifold aspects as priest and preacher, philosopher and theologian, catechist and poet, diplomat and linguist, author and futurist, administrator and humanitarian, laborer and actor, sportsman and athlete, world pilgrim and universal champion of the human person? How do you paint a verbal picture of a moral force in the world, a leader of heads of state, a successor to Saint Peter?

You go to the very depth of divinity, to the very essence of being, to the power and meaning of *virtue,* which means strength, and derives from the Latin word *vir*—man. You go to the foundation stones, to the pillars, to the core of a person's relationship with God. You go to the cardinal virtues. You go to love, faith, and hope.

Love, Faith, and Hope

Do not lose heart! Throw yourselves into Christ's arms:

he will refresh you. May this be your Jubilee:

a pilgrimage of conversion to Jesus.

—Speech to the Active Apostles of the
New Evangelization, February 19, 2000

John Paul II was a man of consummate and unselfish love: a love for God and his Church as a Catholic priest who became pope; of a love for the Blessed Mother; of a love for his parents and family; of a love for his country with its Krakow and Wawel and Czestochowa; of a love for his colleagues and school-mates and friends with whom he kept contact even up to the end; of a love for the poor, the sick, the disabled, the disenfranchised for whom he became an eloquent spokesman. And in an extended sense, he was a person of respectful love of literature, linguistics, philosophy, theology, the theater, sports, hiking, and camping trips.

John Paul II was a man of deep and intense faith. His Catholic faith shaped his life from the sacraments of baptism (1920), holy communion (1929), confirmation (1938), and reconciliation—to his ordination to the dia-conate and then the priesthood (1946), and the anointing of the sick (1981, 2005). In essence his was a traditional Christian faith infused with a special millennial Polish flavor. It suffused every aspect of daily life, from a morn-ing offering to a bedtime examination of conscience, from mundane tasks to world-shaking decisions.

There is no question that his faith helped him to accept the early tragedies of his life: first the death of his mother Emilia (1929), then his brother Edmund (1932), and then the death of his father, Karol Sr., when Karol Jr.

was eighteen (1941). That same dynamic faith helped shape his vocation to the priesthood as he struggled with his attraction to the stage and theater. That same enduring faith supported him during his years as a manual laborer. That same inspiring faith guided him through his seminary studies in Krakow (1944–46), his priestly ordination (1946), his graduate studies in Rome (1946–48), and his parish work. That same fervent faith was his source of strength as he was consecrated auxiliary bishop of Krakow (1958), as archbishop and metropolitan of that See (1966), and as a participant in the Second Vatican Council (1962–65), and continued to be the foundation on which he built his twenty-seven years as pope—as a teacher of faith, as an exemplar of faith, and as a rock of faith.

John Paul II was a man of ardent and boundless hope, which was rooted in his love and faith. He lived that hope during the German occupation of Poland during World War II, during the years of totalitarian control by the Soviets and homeland Communists, during the years of Solidarity and the overthrow of the Red regime. Then he placed that hope in God and the Blessed Mother. He had great hope for the future of all humankind, for peace and justice, for marriage and family, for children and youth, for his dream of a reconciliation between East and West, and for a new spring of joyous promise and reverent harmony.

The Man

Look upon us, eternal Son of God, who took flesh in the womb of the Virgin Mary! All humanity, with its burden of trials and troubles, stands in need of you. Stay with us, living Bread which came down from heaven for our salvation! Stay with us forever! Amen!

—*from Christmas Eve homily, 2004*

I t all began with a signal—white smoke from a Vatican chimney on October 16, 1978. The secret ballots of the conclave were burned. Cardinal Felici appeared on the balcony in front of St. Peter's and introduced the new pope from a far-away country. "The most Eminent and Reverend Karol, Cardinal of the Holy Roman Church, Wojtyla, who has taken the name John Paul II." He was the third pope the Church knew in 1978. At age fifty-eight he was the 264th bishop of Rome, the first non-Italian pope in 455 years, and the first Polish pope.

John Paul II, born on May 18, 1920, in Wadowice, Poland, was a happy blend of a great variety of qualities. In theology and Church teaching he was a conservative. In social teaching and action he was a liberal. In approaching problems he was a radical, that is, he reached down to the *roots* of a problem. He was collegial in governing, always consulting and seeking advice—even if at times it did not appear to be so. He was open-minded and often unpredictable. His administrative style called for much delegation. He was strong and in control. Like Christ, he taught "with authority" (Matt 7:29). He was confident and unafraid. He was an early riser and a very hard worker. He had a phenomenal memory for people and places and events. In conversation he was a listener more than a talker. He asked endless questions:

"What are they saying?" "What was the reaction?" He had a great sense of humor. The Eucharist was central to his day and his whole life. He was a man of frequent and deep prayer. He was ascetical and humble—upon disembarking from an airplane, he used to kneel to kiss the ground of a new country he would visit. He was a blend of the rational West (mind) and the romantic East (heart). He often spoke of his personal weakness, his reliance on the Holy Spirit, and his dependence on God's grace. His motto came from Thomas à Kempis's *Imitation of Christ* (Bk. III, 5, 3): *"Deus meus, amor meus, tu totus meus et ego totus tuus"* (My God, my love, you are all mine and I am totally yours). He was a person of great diversity. He prayed and, until his mid-seventies, he skied. He wrote encyclicals and he used to hike through the mountains. He composed poetry and kissed babies. He received heads of state and dined with prisoners. He canonized saints and absolved sinners. He was a man of God and a man of the people. He could be serious and he could be witty. He was steeped in Holy Scripture, had an exhaustive knowledge of Polish and European literature, and cultivated a rich and complicated literary style. Ultimately, he was a man of deep virtue.

For the entire length of his pontificate he reached out to the faithful of the world, figuratively in message and literally in hand—wide and thick-fingered, the hand of a laborer. Countless photos (there are about three million in the papal collection) depict him stretching out his arms to touch those around him. At any one time there could be as many as a dozen hands trying to touch him. He stretched forth and gave that added opportunity for that one papal touch so many craved and wished for—and received. It was the hand of blessing, the caring hand of the shepherd-pope.

He spoke and wrote millions of words: words of love and faith, hope and comfort, instruction and guidance, caution and castigation, prayer and intercession, greeting and warmth, profundity and reflection, power and silence.

He was a man who knew suffering through the loss of mother, brother, and father; through the humiliation of the German occupation and the persecution of his Church and its churchmen; through the attempt on his life by Mehmet Ali Agca in St. Peter's Square on May 13, 1981, whom he later visited in prison and forgave. He shared the suffering of his fellow countrymen under communism. He experienced the suffering of a broken shoulder (1993) and a broken hip (1994), of a painful knee condition that prevented him from kneeling and standing for any length of time, and of many other ailments. He frequently spoke of sharing the suffering of the hungry poor, the disabled and infirm, the sick, the rejected, and the marginalized.

In his reflective thinking the Holy Father was a true futurist. Early in his writing and in his addresses he made frequent allusions to the third millennium and the twenty-first century. He looked into the future and felt responsible for it. He felt that it was the responsibility of the Church he headed to make a difference in the world, to shape and form that future through its centuries-old teaching and present-day activity. While he was totally immersed in building that future on the rock-solid foundation of the past of the Church and of the world, he was fully aware of the condition and circumstances of this present world. He so longed to live into the third millennium. And he did.

When the Holy Father looked to the future, he saw a new world that had to be built on four basic principles of philosophy and theology. The Middle Ages focused on the centrality of God, while the Renaissance mistakenly put all of its emphasis on the centrality of man. Pope John Paul II, without taking any emphasis away from man, wished to replace that Renaissance emphasis on man who is a child of God, his creature, bearing his image and likeness, his child by adoption, the subject of God's infinite love—with an emphasis on man's relationship with God.

This thought led to the first principle: *the person is more important than the thing*. By divine creation the person carries the image of his Creator. He has an immortal soul, an eternal destiny. As a person he has infinite value in the eyes of God. This person must be held in high respect; this person must be guaranteed his personal freedom. A *thing* is secondary and subordinate to a person. We can never sacrifice the person to the thing—whether that thing be a machine, a political system, or anything that dehumanizes the human person.

Second, *being is more important than "having," the phenomenon of a person's existence is more important than all of his possessions.* What he is, what kind of person he is—*that* is important, and not house, or car, or clothes, or jewels. Emphasis on possessions detracts from the dignity of the person and violates the proper relationship between the person, the being, and the value of the possession, the "having."

Third, *morality is more important than technology.* A system of values, a system of laws, a system of rules—ethics—supersedes the products of man's creativity and inventiveness. Technology can bring into being an endless number of new products, new medicines, new procedures, new powers. But the creations of man must serve him; he cannot serve them or be governed by them. If the emphasis is on the proper use of technology and is governed by the rules of a proper ethical system of values, then we have a proper balance.

Fourth, *love must perfect justice.* Every person has a right to justice, but love transcends justice and gives man even more than he deserves, gives him more than he even needs because it gives him the power of personal surrender, the power of sharing, the power of giving. And giving as it relates to person and thing and possession and technology takes both person and love out of that framework and sets him before God, making him God-like in the sense of being a child of God and gives him the right—through love—to be rewarded with his God-gift: heaven.

⚜

The media called him *John Paul Superstar*. He took the world by storm—a one-man army. He was up-to-date and appealed to the young. He was a different *kind* of pope. There was something mysteriously attractive about him. He was so natural, so unrehearsed. A nod of the head in agreement; a hand raised as if to lead a band; a smile—now spreading, now flowing over the lips, now pursing—a frown like a question, like amazement; pain, anguish, intensity.

By nature and history the life of a pope can be a lonely one. Not in the case of John Paul II. He loved having people around him; he thrived on the enthusiastic response to his very presence; he relished the company of infants, children, and youth. At each of the thirteen youth days of his pontificate, "he had the kids eating out of his hand." There was hardly a breakfast, lunch, or dinner without company—maybe just one person, maybe more than 150 cardinals.

He took more than one hundred trips outside of Italy. His pastoral visits to foreign countries followed the pattern and model of pastoral visits made to parishes by bishops in Poland, which last three to four days. During this time the bishop meets with every dimension of the parish, is available to everyone. Why did John Paul II travel so much? To teach and preach the good news and to make Jesus present to the people; to support the people's faith; to call Catholics to the service of the world; and to foster spiritual and human values. He saw himself as the voice of those who have no voice, especially in the Third World.

As an apostle of the gospel, he was not afraid of dissent (as was witnessed in Holland, Germany, France, Austria, and the United States) as he preached the words of Jesus, "Do not be afraid!" and "The truth shall make you free!" He established a successful dialogue with the Jews, was the first pope to visit the Roman synagogue, and established full diplomatic relations with Israel. He was not afraid to admit guilt on the part of the Church and to ask for forgiveness from and reconciliation with the Jews, the Orthodox, Protestants, scholars, and scientists.

A personal warmth exuded from him like the rays of the sun, letting his light shine before all so that they might see goodness in his acts and give praise to his heavenly Father. As proof of his popularity and availability, he received more than five thousand letters each *day*—and they were all answered.

A Word Picture

[The Church] repeats to each one: courage, God has not forgotten you. Christ suffers with you. And by offering up your sufferings, you can collaborate with him in the redemption of the world.

—*Message for the thirteenth World Day of the Sick*

17

Maybe when you saw him the first time, he walked as if kicking up invisible dust. He would trundle into a room or a hall, a slight spring to the body's forward thrust, still carrying the ballast of weight below the waist, head leading the first point of contact, slightly falling forward, half in warm greeting, half in weight of human weakness. A knowing smile dominated his initial appearance—as if he remembered you, maybe in anticipated conviction that he would like you. The apparent contradiction between pudgy flesh and strong lines presented him as friendly, human, common, almost earthy.

His size tended to deceive you. There was an appearance of largeness, but he wasn't very big; he was definitely strong but not overpowering; he exuded confidence but did not flaunt superiority; he was in command but there was no commanding air. His conversation was basic but not curt, expansive but not undisciplined, free but not rampant. His manner was easy, smooth, liquid, each word and thought like a molecule of quicksilver: alert, alive, attached. You never noticed the syllogistic patterns (these he disguised with metaphor and simile, evidence for the jury of your mind) or the theorems of his idea-sequences, arranged like a textbook for easy and memorable comprehension. Every expression on his face—conceived in his mind, orchestrated in his heart, synthesized in the rhythm of his total being—authored a unique communication.

What fun he was to photograph, for as you readied your position, distance, pose, focus, his and your word-exchange selected a litany of facial expressions, each of which was worthy of record on film.

"To nie takie proste, mój kochany" (It's not that simple, my dear) was one of John Paul II's favorite phrases. He often used it in discussion when someone, after considerable delving and prodding and digging and dialoguing, arrived at some general conclusion that was not quite where his mind and perspective and reasoning and understanding had led him. It was too shallow, too peripheral, too immature, or not radical enough, not broad enough, not deep enough. It was too simple. And, as the pope often said, "It's not that simple, my dear." This *my dear* at the end was more than a polite enclitic, more than a comfortable closing, more than a habitual form of courteous direct address. It was a basis for the communication, it was a description of a relationship, it was seal and bond for open, honest, unprejudiced dialogue. John Paul II meant it. The *my* made you his brother and sister in Christ; there was no possession here, no superiority, no authority, no one-upmanship; and the *dear* made you special, unique, possessed of human dignity, to be listened to, appreciated, reckoned with, respected.

There was a certain deliberateness about John Paul II that might disconcert some, confuse others, and deceive the unwary. It was a rhythm of thought, of word, of sentence, of a posture of the body, or maybe only the leg, or just the foot, or the shoulders—now strong and straight, now loose and friendly, now hunched and wondering, now calm and at rest—or the tilt of head, forward to let you know he was listening, or back to register surprise, or back and to the right to express awe, or up to speak wonder, or down and left to tell you he was wondering about what you said.

He was truly poor in spirit and detached from material things. He owned no suit in Poland and had to borrow one for his American trip in 1969. After Canada, where he wore the suit, he changed into a cassock for the United States. After his election as pope, he had no French-cuffed shirt for his appearance on the balcony of St. Peter's, so you can see his bare arms on those first pictures as he extended them to the faithful. He once said that there were two things he wouldn't give up: his watch and his pen. He carried no wallet, and the only thing he ever took out of his pocket was his rosary. Prayer was his food and his strength. His communion with God was mystical. His later self-reflection was eschatological—one would think that he was already living in eternity.

Pope John Paul II's Many Accomplishments

Overcoming evil with weapons of love becomes the way in which *each person can contribute to the peace of all.* Christians and believers of different religions are called to walk this path, together with those who accept the universal moral law. *Dear brothers and sisters,* promoting peace in the world is *our common mission*! May the Virgin Mary help us to fulfill the words of the Lord: *"Blessed are the peacemakers."*

—From homily, the Solemnity of Mary the
Mother of God, January 1, 2005

J ohn Paul opened the papacy to the whole world. His travels allowed millions of people to see him personally and billions to see him on the television screen. He received millions of people at his Vatican audiences and religious ceremonies. He maintained direct contact with the crowds who gathered to welcome him. He opened the Vatican archives to scholars and the world to the financial condition of the Church. He gave up his throne for a "popemobile." He was *Time* magazine's 1994 "Man of the Year" and appeared on its cover fifteen times since his election.

One of his greatest and most important achievements was the globalization of the Vatican and the Roman Curia. He introduced a great variety of members from many different countries to the College of Cardinals and appointed almost all of today's voting members. He named 90 percent of the Catholic bishops of the world. He held five Synods of Bishops and introduced a master plan of action for each continent. He wrote more than fourteen encyclicals, an exhaustive compendium of Church teaching on every modern subject. He also composed apostolic constitutions, exhortations, messages to the world, messages on world peace, and Holy Thursday letters to priests. He revised the *Code of Canon* [Church] *Law* (1984), and commissioned the writing of the *Catechism of the Catholic Church* (1994 and 1997). He attended no less than five Eucharistic Congresses and thirteen World Youth Days, conducted more than nine hundred General Audiences, and delivered almost 13,000 speeches. He delivered radio and television messages in more than fifty-five languages. He emphasized and implemented the role of the laity in the Church and often spoke and wrote on the place, activities, and importance of women. He emphasized the difference between women and men and insisted on highlighting the special gifts of women. He was not afraid to tackle the profound subjects of sexuality, the goodness of the body, artificial contraception, and Mary as the model of womanhood.

As the strongest moral force in the world, he introduced the concepts of the Culture of Life (from conception to natural death) and the Culture of Death (abortion, euthanasia, and capital punishment). Through his teaching he tried to counteract the tendency in the West to banish faith and religion to the realm of private opinion. He wanted to reverse the movement toward ignoring the value of life and the dignity of the human person.

To the four pillars of peace—truth, justice, love, and freedom—spoken of by his predecessor, the Blessed Pope John XXIII, John Paul II added a fifth: forgiveness. In his "Message for World Day of Peace 2002" he said that "the shattered order in the world cannot be fully restored except by a response that combines justice with forgiveness." He also insisted that the new Constitution of the European Union acknowledge the Christian roots of Europe.

America

It is a great joy for me to return to the United States and to experience once more your warm hospitality.

—Welcome address in St. Louis, Missouri,
January 26, 1999

Despite his many trips to the United States and the Americas, John Paul II was often accused of not liking America. On the contrary, the pope loved America and said so repeatedly. He loved its vigor, promise, generosity, and openness. If anything, he might have been disappointed in America for not being more aggressive in championing the dignity of the human person. In 1987 he said, "I come as a friend of America and of all Americans: Catholics, Orthodox, Protestants and Jews, people of every religion, all men and women of good will." He added as he departed: "Yes, America, you are beautiful indeed and blessed in so many ways. The ultimate test of your greatness is the way you treat every human being, especially the weakest and most defenseless. Guarantee the right to life and protect the human person....God bless America!"

Mary

How many graces have I received in these years from the Blessed Virgin through the Rosary: *Magnificat anima mea Dominum!* I wish to lift up my thanks to the Lord in the words of his Most Holy Mother, under whose protection I have placed my Petrine ministry: *Totus Tuus!*

—*From the apostolic letter,* Rosarium Virginis Mariae, *October 16, 2003*

Before John Paul II put anything on paper in writing, he wrote the letter *M* at the top of the sheet. This gesture was symbolic of the place Mary, the Mother of Jesus, occupied in his life, work, and teaching. She was always on top. He was thoroughly Polish in his love for Mary, in his love for the Rosary (he added the five new Luminous Mysteries in 2003), in his piety and devotion, in his love of song, in his love for nature and the countryside, in his hard work, and in his support of women, marriage, and the family. After he lost his mother at the age of eight, he related to Mary as his Mother. From then on he spent much time before her statue on the altar in the baptistery of his parish church, the Church of the Presentation of the Blessed Virgin Mary. For him she was the Queen of Poland, the Queen of the Church, and the Queen of the Clergy. She was always at his side. Every message he spoke or wrote ended with an intercession to Mary.

Pope John Paul II: A Final Reflection

I, John Paul, *servant of the servants of God,* venture to make my own the words of the Apostle Paul, whose martyrdom, together with that of the Apostle Peter, has bequeathed to this See of Rome the splendor of its witness, and I say to you, the faithful of the Catholic Church, and to you, my brothers and sisters of the other Churches and Ecclesial Communities:

"Mend your ways, encourage one another, live in harmony, and the God of love and peace will be with you.... The grace of the Lord Jesus Christ and the love of God and the fellowship of the Holy Spirit be with you all" (2 Cor 13:11, 13).

—*From the encyclical* Ut unum sint, *May 25, 1995*

For the world John Paul II was a symbol of love and faith, of a two thousand-year Catholic tradition of spiritual power, of holiness, of solicitude, of fidelity, and of humility. For many, both Catholic and non-Catholic, he was a source of strength, a beacon of light, an object of love and affection, a fountain of inspiration, a model of courage, a harbinger of hope, a missionary, a servant, and a pilgrim on his way to another world.

A Poem in Praise of Pope John Paul II, The Champion of Artists and Poets

This message that "Jesus Christ is the same yesterday and today and for ever" (cf. Heb 13:8) revealed to man his dignity! It was repeated by the walls of churches, abbeys, hospitals and universities. It was proclaimed by books, sculpture and painting, by poetry and musical compositions.

—*Address for the Special Assembly for Europe, February 18, 1998*

*H*e enters…

White marblesque figure cuts through the invisible air…

Hard heels hammer against hard wooden floor…

Reaching-forth-head in welcome seeks all at once…

Eyes upon all in silent sweeping smile…

Arms fly in all-embracing arrangement…

Like Bernini pillars in Petrine Square…

Same-strong, same-slight-of-sight, same semblance…

A microcosmic grasp…

The words of welcome are well-wishes well said…

The single-file-clergy-phalanx readies for parry…

Of smile, of seeking, of assurance…

A tease, a wit, bright recoil…

Sincere engagement in friendly encounter…

Time for all…message-words…no hurry…

Pedal popemobile-like touch…

"No, jak tam?"…*says so much.*

A Chronology of Pope John Paul II's Life and Travels

May 18, 1920
Future Pope John Paul II, Karol Józef Wojtyla, is born in Wadowice, Poland.

June 20, 1920
Karol is baptized at the Church of the Presentation of the Blessed Virgin Mary.

1942
Karol starts his studies for ordination to the priesthood in Krakow's underground seminary, during the Nazi occupation of Poland.

November 1, 1946
Previously ordained a deacon, Karol is ordained a Roman Catholic priest. He is sent to the Angelicum (Saint Thomas Aquinas) University in Rome.

September 28, 1958
Consecrated as auxiliary bishop of the See of Krakow.

January 13, 1964
Raised to the archbishopric of Krakow.

1962–65
As an archbishop, he is called to Rome for the Second Vatican Council (Vatican II). He helps draft the conciliar document *Gaudium et spes* (The Constitution on the Church in the Modern World).

June 26, 1967
Receives the "red hat" from Pope Paul VI and is elevated to the College of Cardinals.

October 16, 1978
Receiving 103 of 109 votes from the College of Cardinals, he is elected successor to Pope John Paul I (whose reign lasted just over one month). He takes the name of John Paul II. He is the first Polish/Slavic pope, the first non-Italian pope since Adrian VI, and the youngest pope in one hundred years. He is the 264th pope.

January 25, 1979
First visit of John Paul II outside Italy: **Dominican Republic, Mexico,** and the **Bahamas.**

March 15, 1979
Publishes his first papal encyclical *Redemptor hominis* (On the Redemption and Dignity of the Human Race).

June 2, 1979
Second visit outside Italy: **Poland.**

September 29, 1979
Third visit outside Italy: **Ireland,** the **United Nations,** and the **United States.**

November 28, 1979
Fourth visit outside Italy: **Turkey.**

May 2, 1980
Fifth visit outside Italy: Zaire, **Republic of the Congo, Kenya, Ghana, Upper Volta,** and **Ivory Coast**.

May 30, 1980
Sixth visit outside Italy: **France.**

June 30, 1980
Seventh visit: **Brazil.**

November 15, 1980
Eighth visit outside Italy: **West Germany**.

February 16, 1981
Ninth foreign visit: **Pakistan, the Philippines, Guam, Japan,** and **Alaska.**

May 13, 1981
Pope John Paul II is shot during a General Audience in St. Peter's Square by a Turkish terrorist, Mehmet Ali Agca. The papal jeep rushes the pope to Gemelli Hospital in Rome, where a six-hour surgery ensues.

February 12, 1982
Tenth foreign visit: **Nigeria, Benin, Gabon,** and **Equatorial Guinea.**

May 12, 1982
Eleventh foreign visit: **Portugal.** The pope makes a pilgrimage to Fatima to thank Our Lady from saving him from the assassin's bullet exactly one year before.

May 28, 1982
Twelfth foreign visit: **Great Britain.**

June 11, 1982
Thirteenth foreign visit: **Argentina.**

June 15, 1982
Fourteenth foreign visit: **Switzerland.**

August 29, 1982
Fifteenth foreign visit: the **Republic of San Marino.**

October 31, 1982
Sixteenth foreign visit: **Spain.**

March 2, 1983
Seventeenth foreign visit: **Portugal, Costa Rica, Nicaragua, Panama, El Salvador, Guatemala, Honduras, Belize,** and **Haiti.**

June 16, 1983
Eighteenth visit outside Italy: **Poland.**

August 14, 1983
Nineteenth foreign visit: **Lourdes, France.**

September 10, 1983
Twentieth foreign visit: **Austria.**

May 2, 1984
Twenty-first visit outside Italy: **South Korea, Papua-New Guinea,** the **Solomon Islands,** and **Thailand.**

June 12, 1984
Twenty-second foreign visit: **Switzerland.**

September 9, 1984
Twenty-third foreign visit: **Canada.**

October 10, 1984
Twenty-fourth visit: **Spain; Santo Domingo, Dominican Republic;** and **San Juan, Puerto Rico.**

January 26, 1985
Twenty-fifth foreign visit: **Venezuela, Ecuador, Peru,** and **Trinidad-Tobago.**

May 11, 1985
Twenty-sixth foreign visit: **The Netherlands, Luxembourg,** and **Belgium.**

August 8, 1985
Twenty-seventh foreign visit: **Togo, Ivory Coast, Cameroon, Republic of Central Africa, Zaire, Kenya,** and **Morocco.**

September 8, 1985
Twenty-eighth foreign visit:
Liechtenstein.

February 1, 1986
Twenty-ninth foreign visit: **India.**

July 1, 1986
Thirtieth foreign visit: **Colombia** and **Santa Lucia.**

October 4, 1986
Thirty-first foreign visit: **France.**

November 18, 1986
Thirty-second foreign visit: **Bangladesh, Singapore, Fiji Islands, New Zealand, Australia,** and **Seychelles.**

March 31, 1987
Thirty-third foreign visit: **Uruguay, Chile,** and **Argentina.**

April 30, 1987
Thirty-fourth foreign visit: **Federal Republic of Germany** (West Germany).

June 8, 1987
Thirty-fifth visit outside Italy: **Poland.**

September 10, 1987
Thirty-sixth visit outside Italy: **United States** and **Canada.**

May 7, 1988
Thirty-seventh visit outside Italy: **Uruguay, Bolivia, Peru,** and **Paraguay.**

June 23, 1988
Thirty-eighth visit outside Italy: **Austria.**

September 10, 1988
Thirty-ninth visit outside Italy: **Zimbabwe, Botswana, Lesotho, Swaziland,** and **Mozambique.**

October 8, 1988
Fortieth visit outside Italy: **France.**

April 28, 1989
Forty-first visit outside Italy: **Madagascar, Reunion, Zambia,** and **Malawi.**

June 1, 1989
Forty-second trip outside Italy: **Norway, Iceland, Finland, Denmark,** and **Sweden** (Scandinavia).

August 19, 1989
Forty-third foreign trip: **Spain.**

October 6, 1989
Forty-fourth foreign visit: **South Korea, Indonesia,** and **Mauritius.**

January 25, 1990
Forty-fifth pastoral visit outside Italy: **Cape Verde, Guinea Bissau, Mali, Burkina Faso,** and **Chad.**

April 21, 1990
Forty-sixth visit outside Italy: **Czechoslovakia.**

May 6, 1990
Forty-seventh visit outside Italy: **Mexico** and **Curacao.**

May 25, 1990
Forty-eighth visit outside Italy: **Malta.**

September 1, 1990
Forty-ninth visit outside Italy: **Tanzania, Burundi, Rwanda,** and **Ivory Coast.**

May 10, 1991
Fiftieth visit outside Italy: **Portugal.**

June 1, 1991
Fifty-first visit outside Italy: **Poland.**

August 13, 1991
Fifty-second visit outside Italy: **Poland** and **Hungary.**

October 12, 1991
Fifty-third visit outside Italy: **Brazil.**

February 19, 1992
Fifty-fourth visit outside Italy: **Senegal, Gambia,** and **Guinea.**

June 4, 1992
Fifty-fifth visit outside Italy: **Angola, São Tomé,** and **Principe.**

October 9, 1992
Fifty-sixth visit outside Italy: **Santo Domingo.**

February 3, 1993
Fifty-seventh pastoral visit outside Italy: **Uganda** and **Sudan.**

April 25, 1993
Fifty-eighth visit outside Italy: **Albania.**

June 12, 1993
Fifty-ninth visit outside Italy: **Spain.**

August 9–15, 1993
Sixtieth foreign visit: **Jamaica, Mexico,** and **Denver, Colorado,** for eighth World Youth Day.

September 4, 1993
Sixty-first visit outside Italy: **Lithuania, Latvia,** and **Estonia:** Pope John Paul II is the first pope ever to visit these countries.

September 10, 1994
Sixty-second visit outside Italy: **Croatia.**

December 26, 1994
Pope John Paul II is named *Time* magazine's "Man of the Year" for 1994.

January 11, 1995
Sixty-third visit outside Italy: the **Philippines; Papua, New Guinea; Australia;** and **Sri Lanka.**

May 20, 1995
Sixty-fourth papal visit outside of Italy: **Poland** and the **Czech Republic**.

June 3–4, 1995
Sixty-fifth papal trip outside of Italy: **Belgium**.

June 30, 1995
Sixty-sixth visit outside Italy: **Slovak Republic.**

September 14, 1995
Sixty-seventh foreign visit: **Cameroon, Kenya,** and **South Africa.**

October 4, 1995
Sixty-eighth visit outside Italy: the **United States** (New York, Newark, Brooklyn, Baltimore).

February 5, 1996
Sixty-ninth foreign visit: **Guatemala, Nicaragua, El Salvador,** and **Venezuela.**

April 14, 1996
Seventieth foreign trip: **Tunisia.**

May 17–19, 1996
Seventy-first trip for the pope: **Slovenia.**

June 21–23, 1996
Seventy-second foreign trip: **Germany.**

September 6, 1996
Seventy-third foreign apostolic visit: **Hungary.**

September 19–22, 1996
Seventy-fourth foreign trip: **France.**

November 1, 1996
Fiftieth anniversary of the pope's ordination to the priesthood.

April 12–13, 1997
Seventy-fifth foreign pastoral visit: **Sarajevo.**

April 25–27, 1997
Seventy-sixth foreign trip: **Czech Republic.**

May 10–11, 1997
Seventy-seventh foreign pastoral trip: **Lebanon.**

May 31, 1997
The pope's seventy-eighth foreign pastoral visit is back to his native **Poland**.

August 21–24, 1997
Seventy-ninth foreign visit: **Paris, France.**

October 2–5, 1997
Eightieth papal trip: **Brazil.**

October 19, 1997
Pope declares Saint Thérèse of Lisieux, also known as Thérèse of the Child Jesus, a doctor of the Church. She is only the thirty-third doctor, the third woman (with Saint Catherine of Siena and Saint Teresa of Avila), the youngest doctor, and the only doctor Pope John Paul has proclaimed.

January 21–25, 1998
The eighty-first pastoral visit outside of Italy: **Cuba.**

March 21–23, 1998
Eighty-second foreign pastoral trip: **Nigeria.**

June 19, 1998
Eighty-third foreign apostolic visit: **Austria** (his third trip to that country).

October 2, 1998
Eighty-fourth foreign visit: **Croatia.**

January 22, 1999
Eighty-fifth foreign trip: **Mexico** and **St. Louis, Missouri.**

March 1, 1999
Pope John Paul II permits the beginning of the cause of beatification for Mother Teresa of Calcutta.

May 7–9, 1999
Eighty-sixth foreign pastoral visit: **Romania.**

June 5–17, 1999
Eighty-seventh foreign pastoral visit: **Poland.**

September 19, 1999
Eighty-eighth foreign pastoral visit: **Slovenia.**

November 5–9, 1999
Eighty-ninth foreign trip: **India** and the **Republic of Georgia.**

December 11, 1999
Sistine Chapel's complete restoration is finished: pope reopens the famous chapel.

December 24, 1999
The Holy Jubilee Year of 2000 begins as Pope John Paul II opens the Holy Door at St. Peter's Basilica.

February 24–26, 2000
Ninetieth foreign pastoral visit: **Egypt.**

March 20–26, 2000
Ninety-first trip is a pilgrimage to the Holy Land: **Jordan, Israel,** and **Palestine.**

May 12–13, 2000
Ninety-second foreign visit: **Fatima, Portugal.**

June 26, 2000
The Third Secret of Fatima is revealed.

May 4–9, 2001
Ninety-third trip abroad: **Malta, Syria,** and **Greece.**

June 23–27, 2001
Ninety-fourth foreign visit: **Ukraine.**

August 1, 2001
Pope John Paul II holds his one thousandth General Audience.

September 22–27, 2001
Ninety-fifth foreign trip: **Kazakhstan** and **Armenia.**

November 18, 2001
The pope invites all Catholics to a day of fasting (December 14) in response to the terrorist attacks on September 11, 2001. He also invites world religious leaders to a Day of Prayer for Peace in Assisi, Italy.

May 22–26, 2002
Ninety-sixth papal trip: **Bulgaria** and **Azerbaijan**—the latter home to only 120 Catholics.

July 23, 2002
Ninety-seventh apostolic trip: **Toronto, Canada; Guatemala City, Guatemala;** and **Mexico City, Mexico.**

August 16–19, 2002
Ninety-eighth papal trip: back home to **Poland.**

October 16, 2002
The pope composes and promulgates the apostolic letter *Rosarium Virginis Mariae,* thereby creating (1) the Five New Luminous Mysteries, and (2) the Year of the Rosary (to run until October 2003).

May 3–4, 2003
Ninety-ninth papal trip: **Spain** (for the fifth time).

June 5–9, 2003
100th papal pastoral visit: **Croatia.**

June 22, 2003
101st pastoral visit: **Bosnia.**

September 11, 2003
102nd pastoral trip abroad: **Slovakia.**

March 9, 2004
John Paul II passes Pope Leo XIII as having the second-longest pontificate in the history of the Church—only behind Blessed Pope Pius IX.

June 5–6, 2004
103rd pastoral visit: **Switzerland.**

June 10, 2004
During Corpus Christi celebrations, John Paul II announces a Eucharistic Year starting in October 2004 and ending in October 2005.

August 14–15, 2004
104th papal trip: **Lourdes, France.** Celebrates the 150th anniversary of the dogma of the Immaculate Conception of the Blessed Virgin Mary.

October 16, 2004
Begins his twenty-seventh year of papacy.

April 2, 2005
Pope John Paul II dies. Over three million people converge on Rome to pay homage.

DATE DUE
